INTRODUCTION

I've written this book to lead you to the true
source of all calm. That source is found in none
other than Jesus Christ. It is through him that you
can ultimately obtain peace in a peaceless world.

Throughout this little book you will find priceless
gems of spiritual advice and comfort to help you face
the challenges of each day. It is God's will that none
of his children become perplexed with the cares and
toils of life, for he is more than willing to cover you
with his calming presence.

Open this book at any page and claim those
precious promises that will bring ultimate peace
and calm to your life.

Richard Daly

KNOW GOD, KNOW CALM ...
NO GOD, NO CALM

The secret of being calm is knowing
the God of calm. The more you get to
know him, the calmer and more at
peace you will become within yourself.

Psalm 46:10

LET GOD BE GOD

Anxiety is calm's greatest destroyer ... when we are agitated or frightened by events in our lives, let us learn to let God be God and accept his direction and leading.

Proverbs 16:3
Philippians 4:6

SEEK WISDOM

There is security and rest in the wisdom
of the eternal Scriptures.

James 1:5

LET GOD SHAPE YOU

If you're going through an unusual amount of grief and pain, don't despair. The master potter is at work in your life. He sometimes has to break us so he can remake us.

Jeremiah 18:4

THINK HAPPINESS

Happiness is a product of the mind, of
attitude and thought. It comes from you,
not to you. To be happy you must choose
to be happy: the Scriptures say, 'as a man
thinks in his heart, so is he.'

Proverbs 23:7

INTERRUPT YOURSELF

Sometimes a short break can actually help you get the job done faster. When stress threatens your concentration, take a deep breath, relax your muscles and picture yourself in a calm environment. After you've unwound go back to the job.

Genesis 2:1–2

EVALUATE YOUR DAY

It may encourage you to ask yourself,
'What was the best thing that happened to
me today?' at the end of each day.

Psalm 42:8

BETTER TO GIVE THAN TO RECEIVE

The most important thing about giving is that it imparts values of generosity and thoughtfulness. *Priceless* treasures are usually the best gifts, giving the greatest delight.

Acts 20:35
James 1:17

EXERCISE

If you don't use it, you lose it. That's certainly true of muscle strength. Walking, jogging, cycling or swimming gets the muscles working, the heart beating faster, and the blood whizzing through the arteries. There's the added bonus of a feeling of well-being, produced by endorphins released from the brain during exercise.

3 John 2

CHOOSE TO RELAX

Behaviour modification can help you to live a healthier life. In tense situations tell yourself, 'I can't handle everything, but I am in charge of my attitude, and I choose to relax.'

Psalm 42:5

TAKE JOY IN SIMPLICITY

The nicest and sweetest days are not
necessarily those in which anything
very spectacular or wonderfully
exciting happens, but those that bring
simple pleasures, such as the sun
sinking like a gold coin into the
pocket of night.

Psalm 96:11–12

Know your limits

Those who are happily successful in life are
willing to work hard but know their limits.
For such people work is not everything:
they know how to relax, prize close friends
and spend quality time with their families.

Proverbs 4:10–13

BE INSPIRED BY WATER

There's something about water that has an instinctive, calming influence ... a trickling river, a crystal fountain, the vast open sea, a gushing waterfall or a tranquil lake – such wonders of nature ought to inspire you with calm and awe.

Psalm 137:1

LISTEN TO YOUR BODY

God in his ingenious, creative design for
humankind, has built within us natural alarm
signals – headaches, exhaustion, migraine,
stress, agitation – to warn us when the
pendulum of calm has swung too far. Do
yourself a favour and listen to your body.

Psalm 32:8

WRAP YOURSELF IN GOD'S LOVE

Take God's comfort blanket of unfailing,
unlimited and unconditional love. Then wrap
it snugly around yourself and enjoy the
warmth and protection it offers.

Romans 8:35

STAY IN TOUCH

During times of void stay in touch with
God: he will fill the holes of our emptiness
with his calming presence.

Jeremiah 33:3
Isaiah 26:3

WALK BY FAITH

Each day begin your walk in the calm trust
that God is at work in everything.

Lamentations 3:23
Proverbs 3:5–6

MEDITATE

Most of the time our minds are like water
whipped into waves by the distraction and
pressures of life. We spend much of our
lives in touch only with the choppy surface.
Meditation enables us to calm down, so the
water becomes clear and still.

Psalm 104:34
Psalm 19:14

TAKE SHELTER WITH GOD

In the stormy periods of life God promises,
'When you pass through the waters I will
be with you; and through the rivers they
shall not overflow you.' With him you can
weather any storm.

Isaiah 43:2

SOMEONE'S THINKING ABOUT YOU

God thinks about us all the time; he says, 'I know the thoughts I have toward you ... thoughts of peace and not of evil, thoughts to give you hope and a future.'

Jeremiah 29:11

BASK IN THE COUNTRYSIDE

Picturesque landscapes – the rolling meadow, the open fields, the green hills – all add to the preservation of tranquillity. That's where God leads … 'He makes me lie down in green pastures, he leads me beside still waters, he restores my soul.' How calming!

Psalm 23:1–3

DON'T WORRY!

You can't control the past, but you can
ruin a perfectly good present by
worrying about the future.

Philippians 4:6–7

RATIO 1:100

For every one thing that goes
wrong in our lives, we have more
than a hundred blessings.

Psalm 107:38
Psalm 146:5–6

TAKE GOD'S PEACE

No human wisdom can explain God's
calming peace. It is a 'peace which
passes all knowledge and
understanding'; it cannot be fathomed,
or scientifically explained, but it will
'guard your heart and mind'.

Philippians 4:7

LOOK TO THE LIGHT

It never hurts your eyesight to look
on the bright side of life!

Micah 7:7
Titus 2:13

SEEK THE GOD OF PEACE

True peace comes first by knowing
the God of peace and then by
being at peace with him.

Romans 5:1

TAKE GOD'S STRENGTH

Whatever the circumstance, whatever the price, whatever the sacrifice, his strength will be your strength in your time of need.

Psalm 32:7
Jeremiah 16:19

KEEP PRAYING

A lot of kneeling keeps one
in good standing.

Colossians 4:2
James 5:15–16

COUNT YOUR BLESSINGS

Although pain is inevitable,
misery is optional. We can
either count calamities or we
can count blessings.

Malachi 3:10

REACH OUT

Use what you have to enrich the lives
of others and you will soon find your
own cup running over with joy.

Luke 6:38

CAST YOUR BURDENS

When you cast your burdens on the Lord,
he will not only sustain you but will replace
them with the sweet experience of calm.

Psalm 55:22
Matthew 11:28–30

BE STILL

He who calmed the troubled sea is
more than able to say to your storm,
'Peace, be still.' What assurance!

Mark 4:39
Psalm 107:29

LET JESUS IN

When Jesus comes into your life he
brings the calmness of heaven.

Matthew 11:28
Psalm 29:11

PRAY SINCERELY

To every sincere prayer he answers,
'Here I am.' What an awesome God!

Isaiah 58:9
Psalm 145:18–19

CHOOSE THE FOREVER FRIEND

We are never alone, whether we choose him or not: in Jesus we have a forever-faithful friend.

Proverbs 18:24
Psalm 119:90

BE SAFE IN HIS PRESENCE

One of the characteristics of God is his omnipresence ... the ability to be everywhere at any time. Be assured, then, that though circumstances may separate us from our friends, no circumstance or distance can separate us from the heavenly comforter.

Psalm 139:7–10

BELIEVE AND RECEIVE

Rest in the fact that God's compassion and love never change. Jesus said, 'Whatever you ask for in prayer believe that you have received it and it will be yours.'

Mark 11:24

Appreciate Each New Day

Every day is a gift from God; there are so many potential joys that lie ahead. The Psalmist says, 'This is the day that the Lord has made, let us rejoice and be glad in it!'

Psalm 118:24

GET READY!

If you have been under attack lately, get ready; God is about to show you what the fight was all about.

Psalm 27:14

GO TO CHURCH!

A survey conducted over a period of 28 years
concluded that people who attend church
enjoy better health, have lower blood pressure,
less depression and stronger immunity to
disease! Going to church can't be that bad.

1 Chronicles 16:25–29
Psalm 122:1

AVOID EMOTIONAL BURNOUT

It is not work that wears people out, but
sadness, anxiety and worry. To God all
your griefs are worthy of consideration.

Philippians 4:6–7
1 Peter 5:7

PUT GOD FIRST

The secret of fruitfulness is giving God the first part of every day, the first consideration in every decision and the first place in your life. Try it and see what happens.

Matthew 6:33

DO UNTO OTHERS

Once in a while we all need to hear somebody say, 'I think you're wonderful.' Encourage someone with these words today.

Romans 12:10
Ephesians 4:32

KEEP FOCUSED

If you want to be miserable, focus on what others have and forget what God's given you. Contentment is not getting what you want; it is enjoying what you've got.

Hebrews 13:5
1 Timothy 6:8

BE HUMBLE

Learning to be humble will turn things around in your life when nothing else works. Consider these words: 'Humble yourself in the sight of the Lord and he will lift you up.'

James 4:10

AVOID NEEDLESS PAIN

An inspired composer wrote, 'Oh, what peace we often forfeit, oh, what needless pain we bear, all because we do not carry everything to God in prayer.'

Philippians 4:6
Jeremiah 29:12

PRAISE HIM!

To praise is an exhilarating experience. Go ahead;
get over your inhibition, open your heart, lift up
your hands and begin to praise him.

Habakkuk 3:18
Psalm 51:8

SHALOM

Jewish people greet one another with the word *shalom*. It means 'peace', 'well-being' and 'wholeness'. Your heavenly Father is actually called *Jehovah-Shalom*, 'The Lord is my peace.' The assurance is that God lives up to his name.

Genesis 22:14
Isaiah 9:6

LIVE GOD'S TODAY

We spend so much of our lives worrying
about yesterday and tomorrow, yet one's
buried and the other's unborn. Both are
beyond our control ... but remember
God is 'a very present help'.

Psalm 46:1

WALK BY FAITH

When in faith we take hold of his strength
he will change, wonderfully change, the
most hopeless, discouraging outlook.

Psalm 37:39–40
Psalm 62:8

TELL IT AS IT IS

He who numbers the hair on your head is not indifferent to your needs. Take everything to him that perplexes your mind – nothing is too great for him to deal with.

Matthew 10:29–32

GO TO THE GREAT PHYSICIAN

There's not a sorrow, nor a grievance, nor a human weakness for which God has not provided a remedy. Our heavenly Father has a thousand unknown ways to provide for us.

Jeremiah 33:3
Isaiah 65:24
Genesis 18:14

TRUST AND OBEY

Our task is not to decipher exactly how all
of life's pieces fit together and what they
mean, but to remain faithful and obedient
to the God who knows all mysteries.

Ephesians 1:9
Mark 4:11

LEAVE IT TO GOD

Are you dealing with a difficult
situation today? Ask God for guidance
... then leave the outcome to him.

Proverbs 4:11–12
John 16:13

SEEK ROSES AMONGST THORNS

We all need to become like avid rose gardeners, hunting for buds of beauty within our thorny circumstances. It's a sure cure for complaining.

Genesis 1:31
Psalm 90:17

ACCEPT GOD'S SACRIFICE

The joyful message of the gospel is that
God through Jesus' sacrifice on Calvary
has made it possible for our sins to be
completely forgiven.

John 3:16
Isaiah 1:18

JUST TRUST HIM

If in our difficulties we trust in the
Lord as our strength, he will do
even more than give emotional
relief: he will enable us to rejoice.

1 Corinthians 10:13

THINK WHAT GOD THINKS

When we have done our best to serve the Lord, a thoughtless or critical remark can take away our joy. When that happens you must focus instead on what God thinks about you.

1 Samuel 16:7

AFFIRM

Words of affirmation will always create an
atmosphere in your home that's conducive to
calm and repose.

Titus 3:8

BE POSITIVE

It takes less energy to say something positive
than it does to say something negative. In fact,
doctors now say that when we speak positive
words our bodies relax and the blood flow
actually increases to our brain – and a well-
oxygenated brain will always help us to
handle situations more effectively.

Colossians 4:6

DEPOSIT LOVE

Relationships are like bank accounts:
they're either in deficit, or in balance, or in
surplus. No deposit ... no return!

1 John 4:7, 11
Jude 25

FEAR NOT

The words 'fear not' are used 365 times in the Bible. That means there's a 'fear not' for every day of the year.

Isaiah 41:10
2 Timothy 1:7

YOUR GUARDIAN ANGEL

Did you know you have a guardian angel
keeping protective watch over you each day
and night? The Scriptures say, 'He shall
give his angels charge over you, to keep
you in all your ways.'

Psalm 91:11

TAKE GOD'S INSURANCE POLICY

You have a divine insurance policy that
guarantees complete coverage against fire, flood,
and death. He promises that even though you
walk through the valley of the shadow of death
you will fear no evil, for he is with you.

Psalm 23:4

BE TOUCHED BY THE MASTER DESIGNER

Psychiatrists say our behaviour is determined by our parents and by our environment. But when Jesus becomes the Lord of your life, neither nature nor nurture can prevent you from becoming the object of beauty he intends you to be.

Jeremiah 18:4–6

SEEK GOD'S WISDOM

We can say with confidence that while God's purposes and plans are very different from ours he is infinitely wiser than we are and his timing is always perfect.

2 Samuel 7:28–29

LET GOD SOLVE IT

God knows you better than you know
yourself, and he can do for you that which
you can't do for yourself.

Psalm 139:4
John 21:17

YOU'RE NOT ALONE

You're not alone today. He promised to be
with you through the darkest night. He'll
rock you to sleep in the bosom of his love
and cradle you in the palm of his hand.
Even when others turn their backs on you,
he will never leave you nor forsake you.
Aren't you glad you have him?

Psalm 50:15
Genesis 28:15

Don't Be Afraid

If you're afraid of the future, just check the past. Has he ever failed you? No ... and he never will.

Joshua 21:45
Joshua 1:5

WAIT ON THE LORD

A stress-filled mind always makes it harder
to hear what God's saying to you. So just
wait in his presence. When the time's right
he'll give you clear direction.

Psalm 27:14
Isaiah 40:31

CHANGE YOUR ATTITUDE

Our greatest discovery is that we can alter
our lives by altering our attitudes ... It's
your thought life, not your circumstances,
that determines your happiness.

Philippians 2:5

DON'T QUIT

We're all fighting a battle of some kind, but some are not winning! Winners have one thing in common: a strong faith that refuses to quit.

1 Timothy 6:12
Joshua 23:10

HAVE FAITH

Faith is a walk in the dark with your hand firmly planted in the hand of God whom you cannot see. It is determining to trust God even though he has not answered all your questions. Such faith will inevitably lead to peace of mind.

2 Corinthians 5:7

LOOK OUT!

Whatever you're facing today,
never for one minute think that
you can't cope. When you've run
out of strength and can't fight on,
God will send reinforcements ... so
start looking for them!

Psalm 16:8

SEIZE THE MOMENT

Today there are opportunities all around you to make a difference in the lives of others ... seize them!

1 Thessalonians 5:11

CLIMB HIGHER

Be like the hawk: when it's attacked by crows it doesn't counter-attack. That would be unproductive! No, it simply soars higher and higher, until the pests leave it alone. Lighten your challenges by soaring higher on wings of faith.

Isaiah 40:31

ENCOURAGE ONE ANOTHER

If you meet somebody today who needs encouragement, go ahead and give it to them – more people die of broken hearts than swelled heads.

Hebrews 10:25
1 Thessalonians 5:11

CLAIM GOD'S LOVE

Many descriptions of God given to us in Scripture depict him as infinitely loving and kind. His love 'always hopes, always perseveres ... it never fails.'

1 Corinthians 13:7–8

You'll never walk alone

If you're struggling on your own to face the challenges, then you need to know you're not alone! 'The God of all comfort is with you.'

2 Corinthians 1:3

APPRECIATE SMALL THINGS

It's the little things which reveal the chapters
of the heart – the little attentions, small
incidences and simple acts of kindness that
make up the sum of life's happiness.

Luke 16:10

YOUR UNSEEN HELPER

Who knows how many times the
Lord quietly protects us, redirects us
or leads us on safer paths?

Psalm 23:3

KEEP THE COMMANDMENTS

The Ten Commandments still have their place. The first four enhance our relationship with God, while the last six helps us to love other people. Obeying God's law leads to ultimate calm.

Matthew 22:37–40
Exodus 20:3–17

Use your secret weapon

Secret prayer is your powerful tool against life's conflicts – it provides you with divine rays of light to strengthen and sustain you in the dark hours of life.

1 John 5:14
Matthew 21:22

STEP OUT IN FAITH

The best thing about the future is that
it is offered to you a day at a time ...
though you may not know what the
future holds you can calmly say, 'I
know who holds the future.'

Revelation 1:8
James 4:14–15

QUIET THINGS

Just quiet things – a serene stream,
sweet-scented dusk, the gentle rain, the
hush before the morning bird first
sings – can all fill the soul with deep
contentment and peace.

Isaiah 32:18

SMILE!

Whereas depressive moods can negatively affect the flow of blood in the brain, smiling people produces anti-stress hormones which are an ingredient of calm.

Proverbs 17:22

TAKE A WALK

Physical activity, which helps to relax the muscles and generate a healthy 'glow', can be achieved simply by a brisk 15-minute lunchtime walk.

3 John 2

ENJOY THE FRAGRANCE OF FLOWERS

So sensitive are the human nervous system, mood and temperament, that flowers may stimulate metabolic changes. They bring refreshment and raise the spirits. Enjoy their fragrance and calming beauty.

Songs 4:13–14

SLEEP WELL

The way we handle our emotions has a lot to do
with how well we sleep. An internal clock known
as the circadian rhythm controls the process of
assimilation and body metabolism. Sleep is
important for good health and a calm nature.

Proverbs 3:24
Ecclesiastes 5:12

AVOID NOISY PLACES

Eighty decibels (from a loud radio or snoring) can induce pain, is hazardous to heart patients and can cause stress. There is such a thing as constructive silence: it conserves vital energy.

Ecclesiastes 3:7

BREATHE FRESH AIR

Fresh air provides you with 60 per cent of
your energy. Breathe a few deep breaths ...
then slowly exhale all your worries away.

Jeremiah 30:17
3 John 2

ACCEPT CHRIST'S REST

Rest is the essence of calm. That's why Jesus
said, 'Come unto me and I will give you rest.'
Being with Jesus ultimately leads to calm.

Matthew 11:28
Psalm 37:7

PROMISES, PROMISES!

The Scriptures contain over 3000
promises of help – more than
enough to meet every human need.

2 Corinthians 1:20
Joshua 23:14

DON'T RELIVE PAST MISTAKES

Do not be perturbed about past mistakes and sins. Jesus, your ever-forgiving friend, promises that he will separate them from you as far as the east is from the west. When you remind God of some past sin he responds, 'What sin?'

Psalm 103:12

LOOK AHEAD

We may see much that discourages us.
The forces of evil seem to be in control.
But if by faith we look beyond the
present and focus on the wonderful home
God has prepared for us, we will find
much reason to rejoice.

2 Peter 3:13

A MIGHTY GOD

Though he holds up the world and
rules over the affairs of the universe
... nothing that troubles our peace is
too small for him to notice.

Psalm 59:16
Isaiah 54:10

HE'S ALIVE

Our greatest comfort in life is to
know that Jesus is alive!

Mark 16:6

BE OF GOOD CHEER

The shortest verse in the Bible, 'Jesus wept,' provides us with the greatest insight: we have a friend who has experienced all the griefs and pain that we experience today.

John 11:35
Mark 1:41

LET BYGONES BE BYGONES

To hold a grudge is like sprinkling salt on an open wound. Let bygones be bygones and experience the healing effect of calm.

Luke 11:4
Luke 6:37

SLOW DOWN

Don't get caught up in the so-called rat-race of life. Next time you go out, purposely slow down or stop if you need to: let the handiwork of nature declare to you the glory of God.

Psalm 19:1

BE CHRIST-CENTRED

Don't allow circumstances in life to control
you: be Christ-centred, so that he can
control the circumstances in your life.

Isaiah 42:16
Nahum 1:7

AVOID LATE NIGHTS

'Early to bed, early to rise' is an old-fashioned formula for stress-free living. Try relinquishing this routine: you may find that the principle behind it still works.

Mark 1:35
Proverbs 6:10

SEEK RECONCILIATION

Letting the sun go down on your wrath is a
precursor for insomnia; the better option is
to endeavour to seek reconciliation. With
that purpose in mind you will already
experience the engulfing effect of calm.

Ephesians 4:26
2 Corinthians 5:18

LET GOD TAKE CONTROL

He who numbers the very hairs on your
head does not fail to notice your moment
of need. To him all your disappointments
are his appointments.

Matthew 10:30
Deuteronomy 31:8

THINK HIGHLY OF YOURSELF

In God's estimate you are the 'apple of his eye': his thoughts toward you are as though you are the only person living in the world. What an awesome God!

Zechariah 2:8

CLAIM THE RICHES

As a child of God, you are an heir to his kingdom. That means you also share in his inheritance ... which means whatever belongs to God belongs to you! He promises, 'I will supply all your needs according to my riches in heaven.'

Galatians 4:7
Hebrews 9:15
Philippians 4:19

DON'T FORGET GOD'S BLESSINGS

Take comfort. We have nothing to fear for the future, unless we forget the way the Lord has led us in the past.

Proverbs 16:3

TAKE SIDES WITH GOD

Few things are more intimidating than our fears and our worries, especially when we face them in our own strength. Be assured of this promise: 'If God is for us who can be against us?'

Romans 8:31

ACCEPT THE CHALLENGE

God is never at a loss to know what he's
going to do in any given situation. He
knows perfectly well what is best for us
– our challenge is simply to trust him.

Proverbs 3:5–6
Psalm 62:8

LET GOD HANDLE IT

When you face an impossibility, leave it in the hands of the specialist. He won't necessarily handle it your way, but he'll handle it. 'The things that are impossible to us are possible with God.'

Luke 1:37
Luke 18:27

PASS THE BUCK

When you see the beginning of anxiety ... at
that precise moment pass it on to the Lord.

Psalm 55:22

UNTIE THE KNOTS

Worry drains our energy and makes us tired.
Untie those knots of anxiety with the settled
assurance that the Holy Spirit is your
comforter and guide.

John 14:26

DON'T GET STRANGLED

Our English word 'worry', is from the Dutch *worgen*, which means, 'to strangle'. Worry, if allowed to persist, will strangle us to death!

Philippians 4:6–7
Matthew 6:25–31

BE PATIENT

Those who wait on the Lord
will gain new strength. But
remember: the key to the
Lord's strength is waiting.

Isaiah 40:29–31

LISTEN

The best part of praying is being
still long enough to listen.

Psalm 17:6
2 Samuel 22:7

LET YOUR WEAKNESS BE YOUR STRENGTH

The weaker and more helpless you know yourself to be, the stronger you will become in his strength. The heavier your burdens the greater the joy in casting them upon the great burden bearer.

2 Corinthians 12:9–10

SEEK REFUGE IN GOD

The Lord would like everyone to
come to him as their refuge for
counsel and for comfort. To him you
may tell all your griefs; you will
never be told, 'I cannot help you.'

Isaiah 41:13
Hebrews 13:6

LET GOD BE GOD

God has numerous ways to provide for his children. He says, 'Call unto me and I will show you great and mighty things, which you know not.'

Jeremiah 33:3

REJOICE ALWAYS

Developing a consistent attitude of praise and adoration triggers a feeling of well-being. Take God's advice: 'Rejoice in the Lord always and again I say rejoice.'

Philippians 4:4

SEEK PEACE

True peace is that inner contentment that pervades even in times of adversity. Jesus says, 'My peace I give unto you.'

John 14:27

BE STILL

When all else fails on a stressful day,
just 'Be still and know that I am God.'

Psalm 46:10

LAUGH AWAY

Laughter is release and the best pick-me-up available; so let laughter have its way. Remember, 'A merry heart does good like medicine.'

Proverbs 15:13
Ecclesiastes 3:4

REMEMBER THE SABBATH

Knowing that work and the stress of
life can cause fatigue, God has given us
a special day of rest. It's called the
Sabbath ... one day in seven God tells
us to take time out for him!

Exodus 20:8

MEDITATE ON GOOD THINGS

'...whatever is true, whatever is noble,
whatever is right, whatever is lovely, whatever
is honourable ... meditate on these things.'

Philippians 4:8

READ A PSALM

The book of Psalms contains the most
wonderful words of comfort and reassurance.
Read a portion from time to time – you're sure
to find something that will encourage you.

Colossians 3:16

TRADE PLACES

If you know a real test is coming, talk to the Lord about it; then trade with him. Hand over your fragility and receive his strength and wisdom.

James 1:5
2 Thessalonians 3:3

SHARE THE PROBLEM

If 'a problem shared is a problem halved', then tell it to Jesus twice.

Psalm 17:6
Isaiah 59:1

FIX THE JIGSAW

Jesus is the central piece of life's puzzle. If
we fit him into place the rest of the puzzle,
no matter how complex and enigmatic,
will begin to make sense.

1 John 5:12
Colossians 3:4

ACCEPT YOURSELF

Calm comes with accepting yourself for who
you are. When God develops your character,
he works on it throughout a lifetime.

Philippians 1:6

HAVE JESUS AS YOUR MENTOR

Life is a schoolroom. In it we encounter quizzes and periodic examinations. You can't have a course without tests, but if Jesus is your mentor he will provide all your answers.

Genesis 18:14
Jude 25

SEE FAILURE AS SUCCESS

It is easy to get discouraged over failure. Instead of seeing apparent failures as obstacles, see them as stepping-stones to success.

Job 22:28
1 Peter 1:13

GIVE GOD THE GLORY

Our major goal in life is not just to be happy or satisfied, but to glorify God. If we do this we will be more than happy and satisfied.

Psalm 146:5
Psalm 20:5

BE COMFORTED

It's always comforting to know that
someone is there in times of deepest need.

Hebrews 13:5–6

LET GOD FIX IT

God does not offer temporary relief;
he offers a permanent solution.

Isaiah 54:10
Haggai 2:4–5

TAKE ONE DAY AT A TIME

God gives us just enough light to see
the next step, and that's all we need.

Psalm 27:1
Psalm 23:2

INVEST WITH GOD

Entrust. What a wonderful word! It is a banking term meaning 'to deposit'. When it comes to trials, we deposit ourselves into God's safekeeping and that deposit yields eternal dividends.

Ruth 2:12

RECHARGE EACH DAY

The Lord's unfailing love and mercy
will always continue fresh as the
morning, as sure as the sunrise.

Lamentations 3:22–23

GIVE LOVE AWAY

There's a chorus that says, 'Love is something if you give it away; it comes right back to you.' Try it and see if it works.

1 John 4:11

WHATEVER YOU WISH

Treasure this Bible promise: 'Delight
yourself in the Lord and he will give you
the desires of your heart.'

Psalm 37:4

KEEP A RECORD

Count your blessings one by one. Write them
down; keep a record. You will be amazed to
discover what the Lord has done.

Deuteronomy 28:2
2 Corinthians 9:8

RESPOND CALMLY

Quarrelling can be a major source of stress. Follow the advice of Solomon, 'A harsh word stirs up anger, but a soft answer turns away wrath.'

Proverbs 15:1

BEGIN WITH PRAYER

Begin the day with prayer. Your mind
will be refreshed and you will be
braced to face the day's challenges.

Isaiah 55:6

CLAIM THIS PROMISE

'Be strong and of good courage; do not fear
nor be in dread of others, for the Lord your
God who goes with you, he will not fail
you nor forsake you.'

Deuteronomy 31:6

SHARE YOUR SMALLEST PROBLEM

We sometimes fail to bring our problems to God because they seem so small ... but if they're large enough to vex us and endanger our welfare, they are large enough to touch his heart of love.

Psalm 42:5

HOLD ON

In those moments of deepest despair, take
courage ... 'weeping may endure for the
night but joy will come in the morning'.

Psalm 30:5

IMITATE CHRIST

If we substitute peace for calm, the following
text reads, 'my calm I leave with you, my
calm I give you'. It's this calm and unruffled
spirit, which was so obvious within Christ's
life, that we too can have today.

John 14:27

BELIEVE GOD'S WORD

'For no matter how many promises God
has made, they are "Yes" in Christ.'

2 Corinthians 1:20

FIND QUIET TIME

It's good to have a daily 'quiet time',
an opportunity every day to give God
time to speak to our lives as we
meditate on his Word.

Psalm 19:14
Psalm 46:10

RELAX

God is 'the God of all comfort, who comforts us in all our tribulations'.

2 Corinthians 1:3–4

SEE YOURSELF AS GOD SEES YOU

It's easy to look at ourselves and feel worthless and hopeless. The good news is that your value is established by God's estimate, not yours! Get your opinion of yourself in line with God's!

Psalm 40:5
Psalm 139:17

ENHANCE YOUR SELF-ESTEEM

Don't say, 'I'm not good enough.' If that's true, then you're God's first mistake, and God doesn't make mistakes. He doesn't love you because you're valuable – you're valuable, because he loves you! Let that sink in.

John 3:16

THINK BIG

Next time somebody asks you, 'Who do you think you are?', lift your head, square your shoulders, and confidently reply, 'I am a child of God; I'm bought with a price; I'm loved with an everlasting love; I'm blessed coming in and going out; I'm the head not the tail ... and if you have a few more hours to spare, I'll tell you the rest!'

Jeremiah 31:3
1 Peter 2:9

LIVE IN GRACE

Grace is 'all of God you'll ever need for anything you'll ever face'. He says, 'My grace is sufficient for you'. When you have him you have it all.

Revelation 1:4
2 John 3

LET GOD PROVIDE

One of God's names is *Jehovah-Jireh*, which means, 'the provider of all'. By virtue of this name God is saying, 'I'll be everything you need.'

John 16:23
1 John 3:22

USE YOUR HEAVENLY COUNSELLOR

Medical researchers have shown a correlation between unresolved anger and heart attacks: it seems that people who bottle up their resentment are far more susceptible than those who diffuse it by venting their emotions. You have a wonderful heavenly counsellor who will always listen to you.

Isaiah 9:6
Isaiah 59:1

BLESSED HOPE

There is nothing like hope; it provides calm for the future. So when life hurts and dreams fade, look forward to the blessed hope of the return of our Lord and saviour Jesus Christ.

John 14:1–3